FRENCH BULLDOG
COLOURING BOOK
by TONY CLARK

Copyright 2023 By Tony Clark. All rights reserved.
No part of this book may be reproduced in any form or by any electronic or mechanical means, including information storage and retrieval systems, without written permission from the author, except for the use of brief quotations in a book review.

Printed in Great Britain
by Amazon